D1504931

Fact Finders®

ADVENTURES ON THE AMERICAN FRONTIER

TO THE LAST MAN

THE BATTLE OF THE ALAMO

BY JOHN MICKLOS, JR.

WITHDRAWN

Consultant:
Richard Bell
Associate Professor of History
University of Maryland, College Park

CAPSTONE PRESS
a capstone imprint

Fact Finders are published by Capstone Press,
1710 Roe Crest Drive, North Mankato, Minnesota 56003
www.capstonepub.com

LIBRARY OF CONGRESS CATALOGING-IN-PUBLICATION DATA
Micklos, John.
  To the last man: the Battle of the Alamo / by John Micklos, Jr.
    pages cm. — (Fact finders: adventures on the American frontier)
  Includes bibliographical references and index.
  Summary: "Examines the Battle of the Alamo, including its causes, leaders, and results"—
Provided by publisher.
  ISBN 978-1-4914-4897-7 (library binding)
  ISBN 978-1-4914-4911-0 (paperback)
  ISBN 978-1-4914-4929-5 (eBook PDF)
1. Alamo (San Antonio, Tex.)—Siege, 1836—Juvenile literature. I. Title.
  F390.M65 2016
  976.4·03—dc23   2015007612

EDITORIAL CREDITS
Brenda Haugen, editor; Juliette Peters, designer; Tracy Cummins, media researcher;
Laura Manthe, production specialist

PRIMARY SOURCE BIBLIOGRAPHY
Page 13— John Sutherland. "The Fall of the Alamo." San Antonio, Texas: The Naylor Company,
          1936. www.tamu.edu/faculty/ccbn/dewitt/sthland1.htm
Page 14—Travis, WIlliam, "To The People of Texas and All Americans In The World." Personal
          letter. San Antonio: The Alamo.org, 1836. www.thealamo.org/history/the-1836-battle/
          the-travis-letters.html
Page 17—Federal Writers' Project. The WPA Guide to Texas: The Lone Star State. San Antonio,
          Texas: Trinity University Press, 2013, https://books.google.com/books?id=9bLpCAAA
          QBAJ&pg=PT68&lpg=PT68&dq=%22Who%27ll+go+with+Old+Ben+Milam%22&sourc
          e=bl&ots=Bl-pVJwqou&sig=Q8Lopx38e81f2_MqcqxXYNx2csA&hl=en&sa=X&ei=83tO
          VYrdC7K1sASKiYGABQ&ved=0CB8Q6AEwAA#v=onepage&q=%22Who'll%20go%20
          with%20Old%20Ben%20Milam%22&f=false
Page 25—Antonio López de Santa Anna. "History." The Alamo.org, http://thealamo.org/
          history/index.html
Page 25—Antonio López de Santa Anna. "Letter to Mexican Minister of War and Navy, General
          D. Jose Maria Tornel." General Miguel A. Sanchez Lamego. Siege and Taking of the Alamo.
          Santa Fe, New Mexico: The Blue Feature Press, 1968.
Page 27—James W. Pohl. The Battle of San Jacinto. Denton, Texas: Texas State Historical
          Association, 1989.

Printed in Canada.
052015   008825FRF15

TABLE OF CONTENTS

—— ◆ ——

CHAPTER 1

A LINE IN THE DIRT

Colonel William Travis surveyed his troops during the evening of March 5, 1836. He had fewer than 200 soldiers to defend the Alamo. The former **mission** building now served as a fort at San Antonio de Béxar in Texas. Outside its walls waited an army of thousands of Mexican soldiers. They outnumbered the Texans more than 10 to 1.

Colonel William Travis
leading his troops

Texas belonged to Mexico, but Texans had rebelled a few months earlier. They wanted to become independent. Fighting had broken out. Now General Antonio López de Santa Anna, Mexico's ruler, wanted to crush the rebellion. Santa Anna flew a blood red flag. This meant he would not take any prisoners.

Travis knew his troops could not defeat the huge Mexican army. He had sent requests across Texas seeking **reinforcements**. Would help arrive in time? So far only a handful of volunteers had come.

Travis knew the Mexican army might attack at any time. He feared all his troops would die. According to legend Travis drew a line in the dirt. He asked every man who was willing to stay and fight to the death for independence to cross the line. The others were free to attempt escape through the enemy lines. Every man but one joined Travis in crossing the line and vowing to fight.

THE LINE IN THE DIRT

The story of Colonel Travis and his line in the dirt has become part of the Alamo's legend. There is no proof that it really happened. We do know that the Alamo's defenders realized before the battle started that they would probably die.

mission—a church or other place where missionaries work
reinforcements—extra troops sent into battle

5

TEXAS SEEKS
INDEPENDENCE

Wagons creaked across miles of rugged but beautiful piney woods and **plains**. Stephen F. Austin led a group of families to settle the Austin Colony in what is now southeastern Texas in 1822. This territory belonged to Mexico, but few Mexicans wanted to settle that far north.

Thousands of settlers moved west in wagon trains.

plain—a large, flat area of land with few trees

6

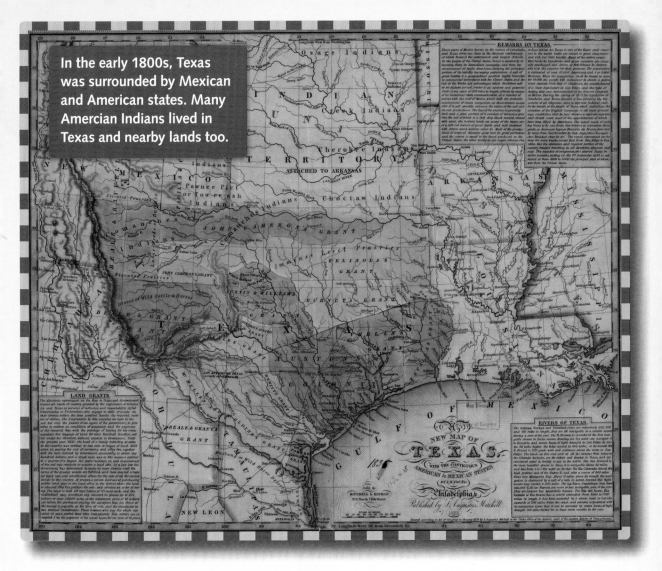

In the early 1800s, Texas was surrounded by Mexican and American states. Many Amercian Indians lived in Texas and nearby lands too.

The Mexican government hoped settlers would develop the territory's rich land. They also hoped increasing numbers of settlers would offer more protection against hostile American Indians. The Comanches sometimes threatened the settlements at San Antonio de Béxar and Goliad. The Mexican government offered American settlers about 4,500 acres (1,821 hectares) of land for less than $100. Over the next few years, about 30,000 settlers arrived from other parts of the United States.

Soon the white settlers far outnumbered the Mexican settlers, called Tejanos. The white settlers brought American culture with them. By 1830 Mexico feared it might lose control of Texas. Mexico passed a law forbidding any more U.S. settlers from entering Texas. Mexico also built forts to watch the settlers.

These acts reflected changes taking place in Mexico. In 1821 the country had gained its independence from Spain. Soon Mexico set up a democratic government. It allowed its territories to largely govern themselves.

Spain tried to retake Mexico in 1829, but General Santa Anna led the Mexicans to victory. He was elected Mexico's president in 1833, but soon he became a **dictator**. He took away many of the freedoms territories had. When one territory rebelled, Santa Anna brought in the Mexican army. Thousands of innocent people were killed. Santa Anna wanted to frighten other areas to keep them from challenging him.

General Antonio López de Santa Anna

As Texas grew, the people living there decided they wanted to govern themselves. They **petitioned** the Mexican government to become a state within Mexico. The petition was denied. The Texans became frustrated. Some wanted to go to war with Mexico and fight for independence. Others wanted to settle the dispute peacefully.

In the fall of 1835, Texans formed a temporary government for the state of Texas. Many Texans still hoped to become an independent part of Mexico. Yet they doubted that Santa Anna would allow this. Most Texans wanted peace. At the same time, they prepared for war. They were ready to fight for their rights.

SLAVERY IN TEXAS

Many Texas settlers came from southern states, and some brought slaves with them. An 1829 **decree** outlawed slavery in Mexico. Mexico wanted to restrict slavery in Texas but found the rule impossible to enforce. About 5,000 slaves lived in Texas by 1836. When Texas gained its independence later that year, slaves did not. The Texas Constitution allowed slavery. In fact, slavery continued to thrive after Texas gained statehood in 1845. Texas left the Union in 1861 and joined the Confederate States of America during the Civil War. The war revolved around many issues, especially the future of slavery. The end of the Civil War brought freedom to slaves throughout the United States.

dictator—a ruler who takes complete control of a country, often unjustly

petition—to make a serious request to a person or persons in authority

decree—a formal order given by a person in power

CHAPTER 3

WAR BEGINS

The fighting between Mexico and Texas started in October 1835 over a single cannon. Mexican troops arrived in the town of Gonzales to take back a cannon a Mexican official had given the settlers as protection against American Indians. The Texans refused to give up the cannon. Instead they fired rifles and the cannon at the Mexican troops, driving them away. About a week later, Texans captured the Mexican fort at Goliad. A revolution had begun. There was no turning back.

In early December a rebel force defeated the Mexicans at the battle of San Antonio de Béxar. Mexican General Martin Perfecto de Cos and his soldiers surrendered and went back to Mexico.

ഇ FUN FACT ഇ

In the early 1800s, Napoleon Bonaparte of France was considered by many people to be the world's greatest general. Santa Anna considered himself a great general too. He called himself "the Napoleon of the West."

Santa Anna (on horse) marched his troops north to put an end to the rebellion.

When he learned of the rebellion, Santa Anna vowed to quash it. He started north from Mexico with an army of several thousand soldiers. Most armies did not fight or move during the winter. Santa Anna marched his troops through cold and rain and mud. Many died or **deserted** along the way. Santa Anna hoped to arrive before spring and surprise the Texans. He wanted to recapture San Antonio de Béxar and teach the rebels a lesson.

desert—to leave military service without permission

11

Meanwhile the Texans gathered volunteer troops. Sam Houston commanded the Texas army, but he had little control over the volunteer leaders in the field. One small **garrison** was stationed in San Antonio de Béxar. The Alamo, a fort that had once been a mission, was there.

Houston sent Colonel James Bowie to San Antonio de Béxar. Bowie arrived in January 1836. Houston considered abandoning the Alamo, but Bowie decided to defend the fort. Its walls were strong. Bowie hoped reinforcements would come before Santa Anna's army arrived at the Alamo.

∽ FUN FACT ⤙

Jim Bowie was famous for his skill in knife fights. The large, sharp fighting knife used by many Texans in the 1800s became known as the "Bowie knife."

Colonel James Bowie was a soldier and frontiersman.

Lieutenant Colonel William Travis commanded the professional soldiers within the Alamo. Bowie led the volunteers. Tensions rose between the two men over who should have overall command. Then Bowie grew very ill. This left Travis in charge.

Travis knew he had too few soldiers to defend the town against a large army. Still, he did all he could to prepare. The Texans strengthened the defenses around the Alamo's walls. They stockpiled food, ammunition, and firewood. Then they waited.

After weeks of slogging through cold and mud, the Mexican army finally reached San Antonio de Béxar on February 23, 1836. "The enemy are in view!" yelled a Texas sentry. The Texas soldiers prepared to defend the Alamo.

Lieutenant Colonel William Travis

garrison—a group of soldiers based in a town and ready to defend it

CHAPTER

4

THE NOOSE TIGHTENS

The Mexican army prepared to lay **siege** to the Alamo. Travis knew he didn't have enough men to hold off the huge Mexican army. The Alamo was a large **compound**. It would take a thousand soldiers to defend it against a full-scale attack. The Texans numbered about 150.

Daring volunteers slipped through Mexican lines to deliver Travis' pleas for reinforcements. His letter on February 24 said his troops would fight until "Victory or Death." This was the same phrase George Washington used during the Revolutionary War.

siege—an attack on a castle, fort, or other enclosed location; a siege is usually meant to force the people inside the enclosed location to give up
compound—a group of buildings often enclosed by a fence or wall

a map of the Alamo area based on Santa Anna's original battlefield map

Only a few soldiers came to his aid. Noted frontiersman Davy Crockett had arrived in early February, bringing a small group of volunteers from Tennessee. Crockett told stories and played the violin at night. This bolstered the Texans' spirits.

On February 28, Juan Seguin, a Tejano, slipped out of the Alamo. He galloped past the startled Mexicans and raced away to gather volunteers to help fight. He did not make it back before the battle. On March 3, 29 volunteers arrived from Gonzales. These were the last reinforcements.

Colonel James Fannin commanded several hundred troops at Goliad, about 100 miles (161 kilometers) away. His troops could arrive at the Alamo within a few days. But Fannin was torn. He wanted to support his fellow Texans. At the same time, he wanted to protect Goliad from other Mexican troops who were nearby.

Finally Fannin set out for the Alamo. The trip seemed doomed from the start. Several wagons broke down immediately. Two days after leaving, Fannin took his troops back to Goliad.

Meanwhile, Santa Anna tried to wear down the Alamo's defenders. His cannons lobbed shells into the fort every day. The Texans knew that Santa Anna would offer "no quarter." This meant he would take no prisoners. The Alamo's defenders knew that they would have to win the battle against enormous odds—or die.

By early March Santa Anna had grown tired of the siege. He wanted to attack. His officers disagreed. In a few more days, their heavy cannons would arrive from Mexico. These cannons could knock down the Alamo's walls and make the attack easier. Santa Anna ignored their advice. He wanted the attention that a clear victory would bring. He decided to attack before dawn on March 6.

A REAL LINE IN THE DIRT

Colonel Travis' line in the dirt may have been only a legend. Historians say there was a real line in the dirt before the first battle at San Antonio de Béxar in December 1835. Leaders of the Texas rebels couldn't decide whether to attack. Ben Milam drew a line in the dirt with his sword. "Who'll go with Old Ben Milam into Bexar?" he asked. About 300 men crossed the line to volunteer. The Texans captured the town. This set the stage for the battle of the Alamo three months later.

Travis sensed the attack was coming. According to legend, on the evening of March 5 he gathered his troops and drew his line in the dirt. He invited all who were willing to stay and fight to the death to cross the line. Anyone else was free to try to escape. Every man crossed the line but one, Louis Rose. That night Rose slipped through Mexican lines to freedom. Bowie was too ill to stand. He had soldiers carry his cot across the line. The Texans were ready to die for the cause of independence.

Travis met with his men before the Battle of the Alamo began.

A FIGHT TO THE DEATH

A sea of Mexican soldiers moved toward the Alamo like a silent wave before dawn on March 6. They killed the sleeping **sentinels**. The yelling that followed alerted the Texans. From behind the Alamo's stout walls, they unleashed deadly cannon fire that killed or wounded dozens of Mexicans.

The fighting was fierce during the Battle of the Alamo.

Sharpshooters killed many more Mexicans with rifle fire. In some places troops had to climb over the bodies of dead friends. The flash of cannon blasts and the cracks of gunfire filled the night sky.

DAVY'S DEATH

According to legend, Davy Crockett fell in battle with a pile of dead Mexican soldiers around him. Many historians disagree. Some Mexican soldiers who survived the battle later reported that Crockett and several other Texans were captured and executed.

sentinel—a person on duty as a guard

Finally Mexican troops reached the walls of the Alamo. Still under heavy fire, they set up ladders and began to climb. The Texans tried to keep them out. They shot down at the climbers. They pushed over the ladders. But they became targets for Mexican bullets. Travis fell to the ground, fatally wounded.

Soon Mexican troops **breached** the northern wall of the Alamo. They swarmed into the fort. Some Texans tried to hold their ground. Others retreated to make a last stand in the chapel.

Fierce fighting raged throughout the Alamo. Overwhelmed, some of the Texans were killed by bullets. Others were stabbed with bayonets or clubbed with rifles. Bodies covered the ground of the Alamo. Historians believe some Texans tried to fight their way through enemy lines to safety but were killed outside the Alamo by the Mexican cavalry.

Men fought to the death to defend the Alamo.

breach—to make an opening or a gap in a structure

The bloody Battle of the Alamo lasted only about 90 minutes. It left dead about 180 Texans who defended the Alamo. About 600 Mexicans were killed or wounded.

As the sun rose, Santa Anna entered the Alamo. A few Texans had lived through the battle. Santa Anna had most of the survivors executed. But not everyone in the Alamo died. Several women and children had hidden in the chapel. Santa Anna released them, along with Travis' slave, Joe.

Santa Anna (right)

Santa Anna described the battle as both a great victory and "a small affair." In the end neither statement was true.

A BRAVE DECISION

Susannah Dickinson and her baby daughter, Angelina, huddled in the chapel as the fighting raged outside. Her husband, Almaron, died in the battle. Wounded in the leg by a stray bullet, Dickinson was brought before Santa Anna. He offered to adopt her daughter and raise her in luxury. Dickinson refused. Then Santa Anna gave her a message saying resistance against the Mexican army was useless. He told her to deliver the message to the rebel leaders, which she did.

#

FROM DEFEAT, VICTORY

As the siege of the Alamo neared its end, Texas formally declared its independence on March 2. News of the Alamo's downfall sent shock waves throughout Texas. But the news of Santa Anna's cruelty made the Texans even more determined to win.

Mexican troops killed many prisoners of war from Texas.

Sam Houston

After the Alamo fell, Santa Anna's army kept pressing forward, trying to crush the rebellion once and for all. Thousands of Texans fled their homes. They took with them only what they could carry. The flood of refugees became known as the Runaway Scrape.

In late March the Mexican army captured Colonel Fannin's force of nearly 400 Texans who surrendered at Goliad. The Mexicans executed nearly all of them. This **massacre** enraged Texans even more.

Meanwhile Sam Houston and the Texans' remaining troops retreated as Santa Anna's army advanced. Houston, however, was simply waiting for the right moment to strike. His troops surprised Santa Anna's forces with a sudden attack at San Jacinto on April 21. Many of the Texas troops yelled "Remember the Alamo" as they stormed into battle. They overwhelmed the Mexicans, many of whom were napping.

massacre—the needless killing of a group of helpless people

Santa Anna fled. Houston's troops captured him a day later. Many Texans wanted to kill him in revenge for the Alamo. Houston knew Santa Anna was more valuable as a captive. In exchange for his freedom, Santa Anna agreed that his army would return to Mexico.

From the hard-fought defeat at the Alamo came a great victory soon after—and independence for the Republic of Texas.

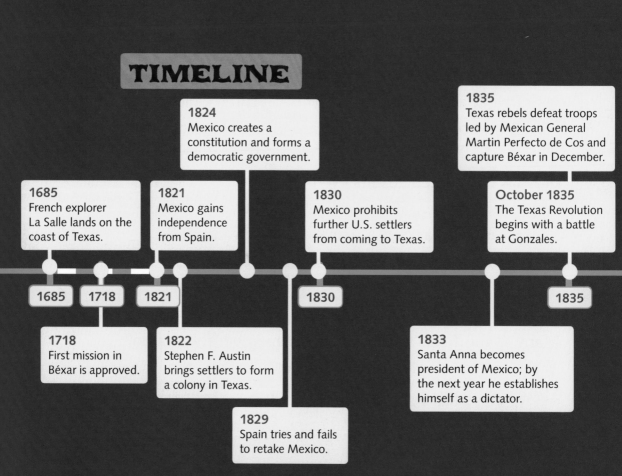

TIMELINE

1685
French explorer La Salle lands on the coast of Texas.

1718
First mission in Béxar is approved.

1821
Mexico gains independence from Spain.

1822
Stephen F. Austin brings settlers to form a colony in Texas.

1824
Mexico creates a constitution and forms a democratic government.

1829
Spain tries and fails to retake Mexico.

1830
Mexico prohibits further U.S. settlers from coming to Texas.

1833
Santa Anna becomes president of Mexico; by the next year he establishes himself as a dictator.

1835
Texas rebels defeat troops led by Mexican General Martin Perfecto de Cos and capture Béxar in December.

October 1835
The Texas Revolution begins with a battle at Gonzales.

Timeline markers: 1685 | 1718 | 1821 | 1830 | 1835

FUN FACT

Today the Alamo is one of the most popular tourist attractions in Texas. Located in downtown San Antonio, it draws more than 2.5 million visitors each year.

March 27, 1836
The Mexicans execute about 400 Texas troops captured at Goliad.

April 21, 1836
The Texans win the Battle of San Jacinto and capture Santa Anna the next day; in exchange for his freedom, Santa Anna promises to withdraw his army from Texas.

June 1836
The Texans reclaim the Alamo.

March 6, 1836
The Alamo falls after a Mexican attack.

1848
As part of the treaty ending the Mexican-American War, Mexico sells the United States a huge tract of land. This land becomes California, Nevada, Utah, and parts of Wyoming, Arizona, New Mexico, and Colorado.

1865
The Civil War ends.

1960
The Alamo is named a National Historic Landmark.

February 1836
Santa Anna lays siege to the Alamo.

1840 — 1860 — 1885 — 1960

1845
Texas becomes the 28th state in the United States.

1861
Texas secedes from the United States and joins the Confederate States of America.

1883
The state of Texas buys the Alamo property.

1846
The Mexican-American War begins.

GLOSSARY

breach (BREECH)—to make an opening or a gap in a structure

compound (KAHM-paund)—a group of buildings often enclosed by a fence or wall

decree (duh-KREE)—a formal order given by a person in power

desert (di-ZUHRT)—to leave military service without permission

dictator (DIK-tay-tuhr)—a ruler who takes complete control of a country, often unjustly

garrison (GA-ruh-suhn)—a group of soldiers based in a town and ready to defend it

massacre (MASS-uh-kuhr)—the needless killing of a group of helpless people

mission (MISH-uhn)—a church or other place where missionaries work

petition (puh-TISH-uhn)—to make a serious request to a person or persons in authority

plain (PLAYN)—a large, flat area of land with few trees

reinforcements (ree-in-FORSS-muhnts)—extra troops sent into battle

sentinel (SENT-uhn-uhl)—a person on duty as a guard

siege (SEEJ)—an attack on a castle, fort, or other enclosed location; a siege is usually meant to force the people inside the enclosed location to give up

READ MORE

Gunderson, Jessica. *The Alamo: Myths, Legends, and Facts.* Monumental History. North Mankato, Minn.: Capstone Press, 2015.

Lanser, Amanda. *What's Great about Texas?* Our Great States. Minneapolis: Lerner Publications Company, 2015.

Pollack, Pam, and Meg Belviso. *What Was the Alamo?* What Was…? New York: Grosset & Dunlap, 2013.

Shea, Therese. *Famous Texans.* Spotlight on Texas. New York: PowerKids Press, 2014.

INTERNET SITES

FactHound offers a safe, fun way to find Internet sites related to this book. All of the sites on FactHound have been researched by our staff.

Here's all you do:

Visit *www.facthound.com*

Type in this code: 9781491448977

Check out projects, games and lots more at
www.capstonekids.com

CRITICAL THINKING USING THE COMMON CORE

1. How does the author support the claim that, in the end, the Battle of the Alamo was neither a great victory for the Mexicans or a "small affair," as Santa Anna had said? (Key Ideas and Details)

2. How does the timeline on pages 28 and 29 contribute to your understanding of the events leading up to and following the Battle of the Alamo? (Craft and Structure)

3. How does the fact that so much information about the Alamo comes from second-hand sources contribute to the various legends about the battle? (Integration of Knowledge and Ideas)

INDEX